So wird es gemacht:

Öffne das LÜK®-Lösungsgerät und lege die Plättchen in den un-bedruckten Deckel. Jetzt kannst du auf den Plättchen und auf dem Geräte-boden die Zahlen 1 bis 24 sehen.

Beispiel: Seite 2
The Auxiliary Verb "to have" and the Present Perfect

Nimm ein Plättchen – z. B. das Plättchen 1 und lies Aufgabe 1:

Bill _____ just closed the window. Find the correct form – "has/have".
Entscheide dich, welche Form richtig ist. Hier muss es <u>has</u> hei-ßen. In der Antwortspalte unter has steht die Feldzahl, auf die du das Plättchen musst. Lege also das Plättchen 1 auf die Zahl 11 im Lösungsgerät. Die Zahl **1** muss nach oben zeigen.

So musst du weiterarbeiten, bis alle Plättchen im Lösungsgerät liegen. Schließe dann das Gerät und lege es herum. Öffne es von der Rückseite.

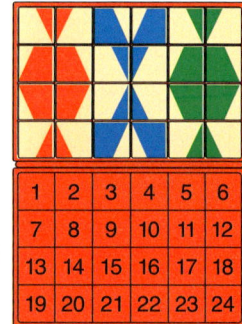

Wenn du das bei der Übungsreihe abgebildete Muster siehst, hast du alle Aufgaben richtig gelöst.
Passen einige Plättchen nicht in das Muster, dann hast du dort Fehler gemacht. Wende diese Plättchen dort, wo sie liegen, um, schließe das Gerät, lege es herum und öffne es wieder. Nun kannst du sehen, welche Aufgaben du falsch gelöst hast. Nimm jetzt diese Plättchen heraus und suche die richtigen Ergebnisse.
Kontrolliere dann noch einmal. Stimmt jetzt das Muster?

Und nun viel Spaß!

The Auxiliary Verb "to have" and the Present Perfect

Find the correct form – "has/have"!

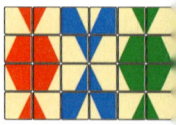

		has	have
1	Bill _____ just closed the window.	11	20
2	They _____ never played tennis.	5	4
3	I _____ always liked peanut butter.	16	8
4	Sheila _____ already cleaned her room.	12	18
5	My mum and my brother _____ just prepared lunch.	1	19
6	_____ you looked at all the exercises?	23	3
7	This sentence _____ got eight words in it.	15	8
8	The firemen _____ helped many people this year.	6	23
9	They _____ even saved ten lives.	13	7
10	My father _____ always wanted a summer home.	20	2
11	We _____ already finished doing our homework.	17	24
12	_____ Alice invited you to the party?	16	14
13	Who _____ already answered the question?	5	21
14	_____ they answered the question yet?	3	9
15	Our cat _____ jumped on the table three times.	1	6
16	_____ you ever shouted at your parents?	19	6
17	Pam and I _____ often worked together.	3	22
18	_____ he asked you for money yet?	2	5
19	What _____ you got on your jeans?	18	21
20	I _____ got spaghetti sauce on them.	7	17
21	The photographer _____ just asked them to smile.	13	8
22	Why _____ they just walked out of the room?	11	10
23	Mrs. Bumble _____ just touched the hot pot.	18	6
24	_____ anyone ever walked on the moon?	14	2

Yes or No: Short answers and the Present Perfect

1	Has the teacher started the lesson?	Yes,	I have • 5	she has • 11
2	Have you got Sally's school-bag?	No,	I haven't • 7	you haven't • 18
3	Have I got your pen?	No,	they haven't • 2	you haven't • 22
4	Have they offered you money?	Yes,	she has • 19	they have • 12
5	Have the robbers got guns?	No,	he hasn't • 20	they haven't • 15
6	Has Nancy got pink ears?	Yes,	I have • 24	she has • 8
7	Have mice climbed up the wall?	No,	it hasn't • 9	they haven't • 1
8	Have the farmers worked hard?	Yes,	they have • 5	he has • 16
9	Has Harry repaired the radio?	No,	she hasn't • 11	he hasn't • 21
10	Haven't you finished yet?	No,	I haven't • 16	he hasn't • 4
11	Have they laughed in class?	Yes,	we have • 12	they have • 6
12	Has the doctor looked at your leg?	Yes,	he has • 2	I have • 13
13	Have they visited the castle?	Yes,	you have • 21	they have • 23
14	Has the dentist pulled your tooth?	Yes,	he has • 19	it has • 1
15	Has your hamster cleaned its cage?	No,	it hasn't • 9	she hasn't • 7
16	Has Peggy cried today?	No,	he hasn't • 17	she hasn't • 24
17	Have you been good children today?	Yes,	we have • 13	they have • 3
18	Have you been a good boy?	Yes,	we have • 18	I have • 10
19	Has your brother cleaned up his room?	No,	she hasn't • 2	he hasn't • 14
20	Has the cow jumped over the moon?	No,	it hasn't • 17	she hasn't • 14
21	Have they helped each other today?	Yes,	they have • 3	we have • 10
22	Has it started to rain?	Yes,	he has • 16	it has • 20
23	Has that man killed the rat?	Yes,	he has • 18	she has • 23
24	Has your team tried to win?	Yes,	he has • 15	it has • 4

A Hungry Dog:
The Present Perfect with Regular Verbs

Tip: have/has + verb + ed. I <u>have opened</u> the window.

Vorsicht bei der Rechtschreibung (-y/-e/-p):

carry	= carried
like	= liked
stop	= stopped

1 Mr. Rich | to arrive | at the party.
has just arrived • 12   have just arrived • 3

2 His chauffeur | to park | Mr. Rich's Rolls-Royce.
have parked • 20   has just parked • 4

3 The chauffeur | to clean | the expensive car.
have already cleaned • 5   has already cleaned • 7

4 Oh no! A bird | to drop | something on the car.
has just dropped • 11   have just dropped • 22

5 Oh no! A dog | to jump | into the car.
have just jumped • 13   has just jumped • 19

6 The dog | to climb | onto the seat with dirty feet.
has already climbed • 3   have already climbed • 7

7 Mr. Rich | to walk | back to the car park.
have walked • 20   has walked • 15

8 He | to stop | next to the car.
has just stopped • 23   have just stopped • 24

9 The dog | to open | its mouth.
have opened • 15   has opened • 8

10 The dog | to start | to eat Mr. Rich's leather seats.
have just started • 17   has just started • 20

11 Poor Mr. Rich! He | to watch | a dog eat his seat before.
has never watched • 24   have never watched • 20

12 Oh no! He to faint .
have fainted • 9   has fainted • 16

13 A guest to telephone for an ambulance.
have telephoned • 19   has telephoned • 5

14 Some other guests to carry Mr. Rich into the house.
have carried • 9   has carried • 10

15 Someone to ask if there is a doctor in the house.
has asked • 1   have asked • 22

16 Mr. and Mrs. Tower to invite Dr. Sheppard to the party.
have invited • 6   has invited • 10

17 Dr. Sheppard to study medicine for small animals.
have studied • 1   has studied • 22

18 He to work in an animal hospital for 10 years.
has worked • 2   have worked • 5

19 The ambulance men to hurry to the Tower's house.
has hurried • 14   have hurried • 21

20 They to walk into the house.
have quickly walked • 18   has quickly walked • 8

21 Mrs. Rich to try to talk to Mr. Rich.
has already tried • 14   have already tried • 17

22 Dr. Sheppard to touch Mr. Rich's face.
have just touched • 3   has just touched • 10

23 Oh wonderful! Mr. Rich to open his eyes.
have opened • 11   has opened • 17

24 And Dr. Sheppard's dog to jump out of Mr. Rich's car.
has just jumped • 13   have just jumped • 6

The Present Perfect with Irregular Verbs

Tip: „have/has" + Partizip Perfekt
(3. Form des unregelmäßigen Verbs)
(eat) = I have just <u>eaten</u> a sandwich.

1 My Uncle Bob has never ⬚ to be ⬚ to Japan.
been • 9   be • 20

2 We have ⬚ to see ⬚ the TV show before.
saw • 3   seen • 17

3 Herbie has never ⬚ to have ⬚ a bad cold.
had • 14   has • 13

4 Have you ever ⬚ to drive ⬚ a sportscar?
drove • 21   driven • 10

5 The burglar has just ⬚ to steal ⬚ my colour TV.
stolen • 1   stole • 4

6 I haven't ⬚ to do ⬚ my homework yet.
did • 7   done • 18

7 The zoo-keeper has just ⬚ to feed ⬚ the lion.
feds • 16   fed • 5

8 The princess has just ⬚ to take ⬚ her seat.
took • 10   taken • 3

9 I have never ⬚ to hear ⬚ such a loud noise.
heard • 13   hears • 19

10 The detectives haven't ⬚ to find ⬚ the thief yet.
found • 2   finds • 23

11 I have [to be] here since 8 o'clock.

was • 8 been • 4

12 Calvin has [to lose] the keys to his apartment.

lose • 18 lost • 6

13 Perhaps he has [to leave] them at home.

leaves • 24 left • 21

14 Have you [to tell] me everything?

tell • 4 told • 23

15 I haven't [to say] anything yet.

said • 19 say • 17

16 What have they [to do] to your teddy bear?

done • 22 did • 6

17 They have [to give] it to my younger sister.

gave • 1 given • 11

18 Have you ever [to think] about being a doctor?

thought • 20 thinks • 18

19 Have you [to choose] the correct answer?

chosen • 12 chose • 2

20 Has she ever [to wear] a mini-skirt?

wore • 5 worn • 15

21 My girlfriend has [to lend] me her silk blouse.

lent • 7 lends • 3

22 How long have you [to know] the answer?

knew • 19 known • 24

23 The bell hasn't [to ring] yet.

rung • 16 rang • 9

24 Ouch! That awful girl has just [to bite] me.

bite • 21 bitten • 8

"Signal Words" with the Present Perfect

Tip: *Es handelt sich beim Present Perfect meistens um einen Vorgang, der in der Vergangenheit angefangen oder stattgefunden hat, aber immer noch einen Bezug zur Gegenwart behält.*

Martin hasn<u>'t</u> found his key <u>yet</u>. (He is still looking for it.)
"Signal Words" begleiten oft das Present Perfect: already, just, yet, not ... yet, ever never *und manchmal* often, always today, this week, this month, this ...

Find the best "signal word"!

1. My mum has ( ) been to Paris.
   (ever • 16) (never • 21)

2. We haven't done our homework ( ).
   (yet • 13) (never • 1)

3. The Redfords have gone to Florida ( ) winter.
   (ever • 6) (this • 18)

4. My mother has ( ) written me nice letters.
   (often • 22) (ever • 11)

5. I've ( ) written her two letters.
   (already • 6) (yet • 9)

6. The horse race has ( ) begun.
   (just • 14) (yet • 3)

7. Fat Freddy has ( ) bet all his money on "Wild Horse".
   (ever • 1) (already • 2)

8. He has ( ) bet on a horse before.
   (yet • 19) (never • 10)

9. "Quick Pony" has ( ) won every race this year.
   (yet • 4) (always • 17)

10. Look! "Wild Horse" has ( ) overtaken "Quick Pony".
    (just • 5) (for • 8)

11. "Wild Horse" has ( ) been in front before.
    (never • 9) (yet • 2)

12 Oh no! "Wild Horse" has ( ) thrown the jockey off its back.

(ever • 7) (just • 1)

13 Have you ( ) bet on a horse?

(ever • 16) (yet • 3)

14 Look! Fat Freddy has ( ) eaten his ticket.

(ever • 23) (just • 20)

15 Caveman has ( ) been to a race ( ).

(not ... yet • 24) (ever ... before • 11)

16 Caveman has ( ) made five new friends this morning.

(already • 15) (never • 18)

17 Have you ( ) been late?

(ever • 7) (yet • 14)

18 You have ( ) lent me your bike.

(never • 23) (ever • 9)

19 Have you ( ) lent anyone your bike?

(ever • 8) (yet • 12)

20 Has Mary lent you her bike ( )?

(always • 5) (yet • 3)

21 The car salesman has ( ) sold six cars this month.

(ever • 9) (already • 11)

22 That cat has ( ) eaten five mice.

(already • 19) (ever • 6)

23 My cat has ( ) eaten a mouse.

(never • 4) (ever • 17)

24 Haven't you ( ) given a cat catfood?

(never • 15) (ever • 12)

Asking Questions in the Present Perfect

	Question Word	Auxiliary Verb	Subject	Main Verb	Object/Adverbial
Tip:	Where	have Has	you the train	put left	my shoes? on time?

Put the questions in the correct order *(richtige Reihenfolge)*!

1.   2: you   4: when   1: have   5: last   3: eaten ?
   1 4 2 5 3 = 20   4 1 2 3 5 = 24

2.   3: a window   4: ever   1: broken   2: you   5: have ?
   5 2 4 1 3 = 22   5 2 4 3 1 = 10

3.   5: promised   3: has   2: not to tell   1: he   4: anyone ?
   1 5 2 4 3 = 11   3 1 5 2 4 = 19

4.   5: had   1: snow   2: in the last few days   3: have   4: they ?
   3 4 5 1 2 = 23   3 4 1 2 5 = 16

5.   3: the photos   4: taken   5: has   2: he   1: yet ?
   5 2 3 4 1 = 4   5 2 4 3 1 = 8

6.   5: have   2: had   3: you   1: when   4: bad luck ?
   1 5 3 2 4 = 21   1 5 3 4 2 = 1

7.   1: has   3: to Switzerland   2: who   4: been ?
   2 1 3 4 = 5   2 1 4 3 = 10

8.   1: that before   2: why   3: haven't   4: you   5: shown me ?
   2 3 4 5 1 = 12   2 3 4 1 5 = 14

9.   5: your aunt   3: spoken   1: hasn't   2: to him   4: yet ?
   5 1 2 3 4 = 6   1 5 3 2 4 = 20

10.   3: Margret   4: has   1: how to use   2: forgotten   5: a computer ?
    3 4 2 1 5 = 3   4 3 2 1 5 = 7

11   2: a box of matches   4: for me   3: have   5: got   1: you ?
  3 1 5 2 4 = 11   3 1 2 4 5 = 17

12   5: watched   3: TV   2: you   1: today   4: have ?
  4 2 5 1 3 = 19   4 2 5 3 1 = 9

13   3: stupid things   2: has   1: done   4: before   5: Willy ?
  2 5 1 3 4 = 18   2 5 3 4 1 = 4

14   5: got   4: hasn't   2: money   1: enough   3: who ?
  3 4 1 2 5 = 15   3 4 5 1 2 = 16

15   1: gone   2: why   3: things   5: wrong   4: have ?
  2 4 3 1 5 = 14   2 3 4 1 5 = 21

16   3: left   4: already   1: the bus   2: has ?
  4 2 3 1 = 8   2 1 4 3 = 17

17   3: Toby   1: painted   2: his bike   4: again   5: has ?
  5 3 1 2 4 = 4   5 3 2 4 1 = 1

18   5: since   2: Christmas   4: has   3: written   1: your sister ?
  4 1 3 5 2 = 13   4 1 5 2 3 = 17

19   4: Caveman   1: been   2: here   5: has   3: since Monday ?
  5 4 2 1 3 = 9   5 4 1 2 3 = 3

20   1: always   2: a doctor   4: wanted to be   5: have   3: you ?
  4 3 2 5 1 = 15   5 3 1 4 2 = 6

21   4: here   3: how long   2: you   1: lived   5: have ?
  3 5 2 1 4 = 2   3 5 1 2 4 = 23

22   5: from her piano lesson   4: Tina   2: got back   1: just   3: has ?
  3 4 2 1 5 = 4   3 4 1 2 5 = 15

23   2: written   3: the difficult words   4: you   5: have   1: ten times ?
  5 4 3 1 2 = 14   5 4 2 3 1 = 5

24   4: been   5: you   3: for the last two hours   2: have   1: where ?
  1 4 5 3 2 = 8   1 2 5 4 3 = 1

11

Tip: *Das Präteritum (past tense) drückt aus, dass ein Vorgang in der Vergangenheit abgeschlossen wurde.*

I <u>visited</u> my aunt last week.

Put the following in the <u>past</u> tense!

1 The train **?** eight minutes ago.

| arrived | 10 | arrives | 16 |

2 They were late, so they **?** to the station.

| raced | 12 | race | 4 |

3 Madonna **?** in the disco until midnight.

| dances | 21 | danced | 7 |

4 Last summer we **?** around Ireland.

| cycle | 24 | cycled | 9 |

5 My sister **?** Irish folk songs.

| listened to | 1 | listens to | 17 |

6 We **?** while we were there.

| camp | 5 | camped | 11 |

7 I **?** to hitchhike, too.

| try | 13 | tried | 5 |

8 Jackie **?** school five years ago.

| starts | 2 | started | 3 |

9 On Saturday I **?** six video films.

| watched | 8 | watch | 17 |

10 The professor **?** to Caveman a few minutes ago.

| talked | 2 | talks | 21 |

11 Yesterday our cat **?** my goldfish out of its bowl.

| knocks | 18 | knocked | 4 |

12 Hundreds of tourists **?** the museum yesterday.

| visit | 1 | | visited | 6 |

13 James Bond **?** into the water and helped the girl.

| jumps | 16 | | jumped | 21 |

14 The smuggler **?** two days ago.

| arrived | 23 | | arrives | 14 |

15 A reporter **?** a terrible accident.

| talks about | 15 | | talked about | 19 |

16 On Monday the smuggler **?** through the customs hall.

| hurried | 22 | | hurries | 3 |

17 The film **?** at 10 o'clock in the evening.

| ends | 9 | | ended | 18 |

18 We **?** to watch films with a happy end.

| love | 6 | | loved | 20 |

19 The policeman **?** the tourist in French.

| talks to | 16 | | talked to | 17 |

20 The goal-keeper jumped and **?** to catch the ball.

| tries | 19 | | tried | 16 |

21 Mr. Kato **?** a cheque to pay for the dinner.

| used | 14 | | uses | 9 |

22 The tired guest **?** a lot of sleep.

| needed | 24 | | needs | 13 |

23 Yesterday he **?** all the dishes by himself.

| washes | 11 | | washed | 15 |

24 The pupils **?** for the results of their tests.

| wait | 10 | | waited | 13 |

The Past Tense with Irregular Verbs

Find the correct form of the past tense!

1	choose	chooses | 3	chose | 18	chosen | 16
2	fall	fallen | 6	falls | 13	fell | 21
3	run	ran | 13	run | 1	runs | 20
4	write	wrote | 6	written | 17	writes | 19
5	show	shows | 5	shown | 12	showed | 14
6	understand	understand | 7	understood | 22	understands | 3
7	pay	pays | 15	paid | 16	pay | 24
8	take	takes | 2	took | 5	taken | 10
9	hold	hold | 23	held | 1	holds | 14
10	lay	lain | 15	laid | 2	lays | 19
11	fly	flies | 4	flew | 17	flown | 14
12	ring	rung | 21	rang | 15	rings | 18
13	see	saw | 23	seen | 3	sees | 8
14	give	gives | 20	gave | 10	given | 11
15	speak	speaks | 1	spoken | 16	spoke | 8
16	come	came | 11	come | 5	comes | 15
17	sing	sang | 3	sings | 21	sung | 14
18	become	become | 18	became | 20	becomes | 24
19	catch	catches | 5	caught | 4	catch | 7
20	know	known | 23	knows | 19	knew | 12
21	begin	began | 19	begun | 1	begins | 20
22	break	broken | 15	broke | 9	breaks | 20
23	say	said | 24	say | 4	says | 11
24	go	gone | 3	went | 7	goes | 10

Regular and Irregular Verbs in the Past Tense

Choose the correct form of the past tense!

1 My dad | climbed • 8 | climbing • 1 | the Matterhorn.

2 We | went • 10 | gone • 20 | there on our holidays last month.

3 I | stand • 9 | stood • 11 | on Caveman's foot yesterday.

4 Herbie | made • 7 | make • 22 | a mistake on the test.

5 Manuela | trying • 16 | tried • 23 | to make a pizza.

6 Marilyn | puts • 13 | put • 9 | red lipstick* on her lips last night.

7 She | kissing • 15 | kissed • 21 | Martin on the cheek.

8 Martin | have • 3 | had • 19 | lipstick on his shirt.

9 We all | laughed • 12 | laughing • 4 | at Martin.

10 Martin's face | became • 24 | becomes • 21 | very red.

11 He | left • 20 | leaves • 2 | the room very quickly.

12 Marylin | wins • 5 | won • 22 | the kissing contest.

13 We all | rushing • 17 | rushed • 1 | up to speak to her.

14 All the boys | get • 8 | got • 3 | a big kiss.

15 Lucy | is • 19 | was • 5 | very angry.

16 Her boyfriend | wanting • 6 | wanted • 2 | a kiss from Marylin, too.

17 He | doesn't • 15 | didn't • 16 | get a kiss.

18 Lucy | hit • 6 | hits • 14 | him in the face.

19 Elke and Sue | remembered • 15 | remembering • 2 | what she said.

20 Lucy | tells • 13 | told • 14 | him not to kiss another girl.

21 Lucy's boyfriend | say • 4 | said • 18 | something stupid.

22 He said he | forgot • 4 | forgotten • 2 | Lucy was in the room.

23 She | runs • 3 | ran • 13 | out of the room.

24 Then she | rides • 7 | rode • 17 | home with Mark.   *= *Lippenstift*

15

"Signal Words" for the Past Tense

Tip: *"Signal Words" helfen uns festzustellen, ob ein Vorgang in der Vergangenheit abgeschlossen wurde:*

last week, last …, yesterday, ago, in 1986.

1   **?**   Saturday I worked in a departement store.
- Always • 4
- Last • 23

2   My cousin was in Berlin two days   **?** .
- yesterday • 13
- ago • 16

3   **?**   week we went swimming in an indoor pool.
- Last • 20
- Ago • 21

4   Thousands of years   **?**   there were many dinosaurs.
- yesterday • 14
- ago • 24

5   Three years   **?**   my father bought a colour TV.
- ago • 7
- last • 15

6   Our mother took cooking lessons twelve years   **?** .
- ago • 15
- in 1976 • 2

7   **?**   year she started piano lessons.
- Last • 3
- Ago • 5

8   My little sister was born   **?** .
- ago • 17
- in 2000 • 11

9   **?**   she tied my shoes together.
- Yesterday • 19
- Ago • 6

10   Fat Freddy ate three pounds of sausages   **?**   night.
- ago • 21
- last • 8

11   We visited my aunt the day before   **?** .
- ago • 18
- yesterday • 12

12 Bob visited his Aunt Jennifer two days **?** .
- ago • 4
- yesterday • 15

13 The train departed from here three minutes **?** .
- yesterday • 9
- ago • 17

14 I wrote a few letters **?** night.
- yesterday • 19
- last • 21

15 I finished reading the comic book **?** .
- yesterday • 13
- ago • 12

16 The cowboy caught the cow a few minutes **?** .
- last • 3
- ago • 18

17 The silly goose was here **?** .
- yesterday • 10
- ago • 7

18 **?** nobody drove a car.
- In 1850 • 14
- Ago • 2

19 **?** the film star gave six interviews.
- Ago • 11
- Yesterday • 9

20 The **?** time she was in London, she only gave one.
- in 1987 • 6
- last • 5

21 The interview was on TV a few minutes **?** .
- ago • 1
- last • 4

22 **?** year someone said she couldn't sing.
- Yesterday • 15
- Last • 22

23 She sang on TV **?** night.
- last • 6
- yesterday • 7

24 I saw her sing in a film on TV two hours **?** .
- last • 3
- ago • 2

Asking Questions in the Past Tense

Question Word	Auxiliary "did"	Subject	Main Verb	Object/Adverbial
What	did	John	give	Sally?
	Did	Bill	eat	at 5 o'clock?

Tip: *Meistens braucht man "did" um eine Frage in der Vergangenheit zu stellen.*
Did you eat lunch? Where did you eat lunch?

Ausnahme: Man bildet die Frage ohne "did", wenn das Fragewort Subjekt ist,
z. B.: Who opened this window? Bill opened it.

Find the correct questions! *(Vorsicht, eine Antwort ist grammatikalisch falsch!)*

1 Who parked their car in my garage? • 8
     Who did their car park in my garage? • 11

2 Why parked you your car there? • 16
     Why did you park your car there? • 12

3 Did you forget to stop at the traffic-lights? • 21
     Forgot you to stop at the traffice-lights? • 3

4 Had you an accident? • 1
     Did you have an accident? • 7

5 Why not called the police? • 5
     Why didn't you call the police? • 16

6 Who telephoned for an ambulance? • 11
     Who did for an ambulance telephone? • 14

7 Took they you to the hospital? • 24
     Did they take you to the hospital? • 6

8 Lost the passenger any blood? • 13
     Did the passenger lose any blood? • 2

9 Why did Fred put ketchup on his shirt? • 22
     Why put Fred ketchup on his shirt? • 7

10 Did he ever anything dangerous? • 16
     Did he ever do anything dangerous? • 15

11 When sat he in the middle of the road? • 18
     When did he sit in the middle of the road? • 1

12 | Stopped all the cars? • 12

Did all the cars stop? • 5

13 | Said anyone else it was true? • 23

Did anyone else say it was true? • 20

14 | How long did you know he was lying? • 24

How long knew you he was lying? • 6

15 | Hit you another car in the park? • 8

Did you hit another car in the park? • 10

16 | Why not tell you me that before? • 4

Why didn't you tell me that before? • 19

17 | Did Caveman and Kevin see the accident? • 18

Saw they the accident? • 15

18 | Why thought Caveman the other car was a toy? • 15

Why did Caveman think the other car was a toy? • 9

19 | What did he with the other car? • 2

What did he do with the other car? • 17

20 | How far rolled he the car? • 1

How far did he roll the car? • 14

21 | What did he after that? • 3

What did he do after that? • 4

22 | How long shook he the car? • 8

How long did he shake the car? • 23

23 | Who was in the car? • 13

Who did be in the car? • 7

24 | Did a thief really try to steal it? • 3

Tried a thief really to steal it? • 18

From the Infinitive Form to the Present Perfect and Past Tense

Find the right answer!

1 Mrs. Conrad │ to phone │ the police an hour ago.
- has phoned • 4
- phoned • 17

2 My parents │ not to finish │ shopping yet. Come back in an hour.
- haven't finished • 7
- didn't finish • 3

3 Have you ever │ to drink │ hot chocolate?
- drunk • 10
- drank • 20

4 How many biscuits have you already │ to eat │ ?
- ate • 6
- eaten • 12

5 Our lake │ to freeze │ yesterday because it was so cold.
- froze • 3
- has frozen • 11

6 Our children have never │ to steal │ anything in their whole lives.
- stolen • 14
- stole • 8

7 Look! That flowers have │ to grow │ much taller.
- grew • 13
- grown • 1

8 We have good neighbours. They │ to keep │ their garden very tidy.
- have always kept • 5
- kept • 21

9 Mr. Robinson │ to teach │ our class last year.
- has taught • 23
- taught • 9

10 Poor Alice, she │ to tear │ her new dress.
- just tore • 1
- has just torn • 4

11 Be careful Sue, the police │ not to catch │ the thief yet.
- didn't catch • 20
- haven't caught • 6

12 Last week my parents [to give] me a lot of pocket-money.

(have given • 5) (gave • 2)

13 It is Saturday morning. Kevin and Sue [to go] on a picnic.

(went • 18) (have gone • 23)

14 Oh no! Kevin [not to bring] any matches. What can they do?

(hasn't brought • 19) (didn't bring • 7)

15 The last time they went on a picnic, Kevin [to forget] a knife.

(has forgotten • 2) (forgot • 21)

16 They are lucky. Sue [to find] some matches.

(just found • 3) (has just found • 24)

17 Have you ever [to do] anything stupid?

(did • 14) (done • 13)

18 Did those children [to take] some of our apples?

(take • 22) (took • 4)

19 Yes, they have just [to take] 10 green apples?

(took • 3) (taken • 8)

20 Did you [to buy] the tickets for the concert?

(buy • 11) (bought • 19)

21 Nick [to send] a note to Julie on Tuesday.

(has sent • 4) (sent • 15)

22 Have you ever [to fall] down before?

(fallen • 20) (fell • 17)

23 Liza [to pay] for the meal and then went out.

(has paid • 12) (paid • 18)

24 They [to meet] each other for the first time yesterday afternoon.

(have met • 10) (met • 16)

Past Tense or Present Perfect Tense?

1   **?**   your brother   **?**   to New York last week?

| Has ... gone • 14 | Did ... go • 7 |

2   No, but he   **?**   to London on Tuesday.

| flew • 11 | has flown • 20 |

3   Come and eat! Mum   **?**   lunch for us.

| has just made • 4 | made • 24 |

4   Look, a new penny!   **?**   you ever   **?**   a new penny before?

| Did ... find • 3 | Have ... found • 8 |

5   No, but last month I   **?**   a watch.

| found • 16 | have found • 19 |

6   Brenda,   **?**   you   **?**   listening to my CD yet?

| did ... finish • 2 | have ... finished • 12 |

7   Mum is happy because I   **?**   my homework two hours ago.

| did • 24 | have done • 5 |

8   Mary   **?**   a new skirt yesterday.

| bought • 20 | has bought • 23 |

9   Jerry,   **?**   you ever   **?**   Mike this knife?

| have ... shown • 3 | did ... show • 16 |

10   No, I   **?**   never   **?**   Mike this knife.

| did ... show • 4 | have ... shown • 15 |

11   Sandra   **?**   her handbag on Wednesday.

| has lost • 8 | lost • 19 |

12   How much money   **?**   she   **?**   ?

| did ... lose • 23 | has ... lost • 1 |

13 I **?** a wonderful film on TV last night.

| saw • 2 | have seen • 22 |

14 The film **?** about music and dancing.

| has been • 14 | was • 6 |

15 I **?** chocolate when I was four years old.

| liked • 10 | have liked • 18 |

16 Kevin and Caveman **?** just **?** to the cinema.

| did...go • 15 | have...gone • 1 |

17 They **?** to the beach on Sunday afternoon.

| went • 17 | have gone • 13 |

18 My uncle **?** me a Karl May book on my birthday.

| has given • 22 | gave • 9 |

19 Look! That taxi **?** just **?** an accident.

| has ... had • 18 | did ... have • 8 |

20 That's strange, I **?** a gorilla in that taxi an hour ago.

| have seen • 12 | saw • 13 |

21 This soup is great! **?** you **?** the soup yet?

| Did ... taste • 6 | Have ... tasted • 21 |

22 **?** you **?** to the zoo last week?

| Did ... go • 5 | Have ... gone • 7 |

23 Yes, we **?** there on Friday.

| have been • 19 | were • 14 |

24 We even **?** the monkeys bananas.

| have fed • 2 | fed • 22 |

At the Cinema
Present/Present Progressive/Present Perfect/Past

Put the verbs into the following tenses: simple present = sim. pres.,
present progressive = pres. prog., present perfect = pres. perf. and past

1 simp. pres.
Sometimes Caveman **?** modern life at all.
hasn't understood • 4   didn't understand • 21   doesn't understand • 7

2 past
A long time ago Caveman **?** very much.
doesn't know • 6   hasn't know • 14   didn't know • 9

3 pres. perf.
He **?** those days with the dinosaurs.
doesn't forget • 3   hasn't forgotten • 24   didn't forget • 11

4 sim. pres.
There are times when he **?** about the future.
wants to learn • 20   has wanted to learn • 23   wanted to learn • 19

5 sim. pres.
Yes, our friend Caveman **?** to see new things.
loves • 17   has loved • 2   loved • 13

6 past
Yesterday Suzy **?** Kevin about a great film.
is telling • 8   has told • 15   told • 22

7 sim. pres.
It **?** an adventure film with Tarzan.
is • 15   was • 16   has been • 6

8 pres. perf.
Kevin **?** to take Caveman to the cinema.
decides • 18   has decided • 13   decided • 5

9 pres. perf.
Caveman **?** to the cinema before.
isn't • 22   has never been • 11   wasn't • 5

10 pres. perf.
Kevin's friend, Rocky, **?** the film three times.
sees • 1   has already seen • 6   saw • 8

11 sim. pres.
Rocky **?** Kevin if he can go with them.
asks • 2   asked • 5   has asked • 14

12 sim. pres.

They almost **?** the bus to the cinema.

missed • 5   miss • 4   have missed • 5

13 pres. prog.

Now they **?** in front of the cinema.

have stood • 7   stood • 12   are standing • 19

14 sim. pres.

Caveman **?** any money for the tickets.

hasn't had • 3   doesn't have • 21   didn't have • 22

15 sim. pres.

Rocky always **?** some money in his pocket.

kept • 20   has kept • 9   keeps • 23

16 pres. perf.

Oh no! Rocky **?** his money, too.

forgot • 10   forgets • 11   has forgotten • 8

17 sim. pres.

Fortunately they **?** Rocky's money.

don't need • 3   didn't need • 13   haven't needed • 7

18 past

Kevin **?** three tickets four hours ago.

has bought • 24   buys • 6   bought • 12

19 sim. pres.

When they go into the cinema, they **?** popcorn.

smelt • 10   have smelt • 2   smell • 16

20 pres. perf.

Caveman **?** anything to eat since breakfast.

didn't have • 15   hasn't had • 1   doesn't have • 21

21 pres. prog.

The film **?** now.

is beginning • 5   has begun • 7   began • 4

22 pres. perf.

Caveman and the boys **?** their seats.

took • 20   have just taken • 10   take • 8

23 pres. prog.

Look! Tarzan and a gorilla **?** bananas.

are eating • 14   ate • 10   have eaten • 17

24 pres. perfect

Oh no! Caveman **?** through the screen*.

jumps • 12   has just jumped • 18   jumped • 9

* = Leinwand

25

Try it Again!
Past or Present Perfect?

Find the correct tense! Signal words can help you.

1 | I ( ) any silly telephone calls last month.
| didn't get • 23 | haven't got • 4 |

2 | But so far this week I ( ) five silly telephone calls.
| have had • 19 | had • 16 |

3 | James ( ) to Scotland yet.
| hasn't been • 10 | wasn't • 21 |

4 | His older sister ( ) to Glasgow twice last year.
| went • 24 | has gone • 1 |

5 | Mr. and Mrs. Fuller ( ) Mum some flowers two days ago.
| have given • 11 | gave • 3 |

6 | Last year my friend ( ) away when he was in trouble.
| has run • 16 | ran • 20 |

7 | He ( ) back a day later because he was hungry.
| has come • 5 | came • 13 |

8 | Aunt Mable ( ) all her expensive diamonds last year.
| has sold • 23 | sold • 17 |

9 | So far this year she ( ) five super holidays.
| took • 15 | has taken • 9 |

10 | The bus ( ) the bus stop two minutes ago.
| left • 4 | has left • 19 |

11 | We ( ) the bus this year.
| have often taken • 18 | took • 17 |

12 I ( ) fifteen tickets on Tuesday morning.

| have bought • 3 | bought • 14 |

13 Last Saturday a girl ( ) a terrible letter to my mum.

| has send • 6 | sent • 11 |

14 She ( ) my mother I threw milk on her dress.

| told • 7 | has told • 14 |

15 I ( ) such an awful thing in my whole life.

| didn't do • 5 | have never done • 21 |

16 But a few days ago I ( ) lemonade in her face.

| have thrown • 19 | threw • 12 |

17 All the boys ( ) when they saw her wet hair.

| have laughed • 8 | laughed • 1 |

18 But today I ( ) a lot of problems with Mum.

| had • 24 | have had • 22 |

19 My mum ( ) me to my room for one whole day.

| sent • 18 | has sent • 2 |

20 I ( ) anything to eat since breakfast.

| haven't had • 5 | didn't have • 17 |

21 But I ( ) one time yet.

| didn't cry • 2 | haven't cried • 15 |

22 Last summer I ( ) when things went wrong.

| have cried • 14 | cried • 8 |

23 Twenty minutes ago I ( ) my friends playing outside.

| heard • 6 | have heard • 7 |

24 I ( ) to say I'm sorry and then I can go outside.

| have just decided • 16 | decided • 23 |

The "going to" Future

Tip: *"going to" future drückt eine <u>Absicht</u> für die Zukunft aus.*
       Bildung: am/is/are + going to + Infinitive
       (Kevin is going to teach Caveman how to speak English.).

Find the correct form of the "going to" Future!

1   They   are going to watch • 5 / is going to watches • 17   the tennis match tonight.

2   Daniel Beaver   am going to builds • 13 / is going to build • 3   a cabin in the woods.

3   Are you going to play • 2 / Are I going to played • 14   table-tennis in the park?

4   Pete and Jerry   is going to play • 21 / are going to play • 6   a trick on Mark.

5   They   are going to tie • 13 / are going to ties • 7   his shoes together.

6   Sally   is going to be • 4 / is going to is • 18   nice to her brother next week

7   Are she going to clean • 22 / Is she going to clean • 10   his room on Monday?

8   What   are you going to do • 17 / are you going to did • 15   this evening?

9   I   am going to programme • 1 / is going to programme • 4   my computer.

10   Mr. Ryder   is going to buys • 23 / is going to buy • 14   a new taxi next month.

11	The Smiths	are going to go • 18 is going to go • 9	skiing in February.
12		Are you going to be • 9 Am you going to be • 12	on time for the party?
13	My parents	are going to take • 11 is going to take • 21	me to the zoo tomorrow.
14	There	is going to being • 17 is going to be • 16	a lot of snow next month.
15	We	are going to go • 7 is going to go • 15	on a picnic on the weekend.
16	My older sister	are going to cycle • 20 is going to cycle • 12	to Denmark this summer.
17	Her friend	is going to meet • 21 is going to meets • 18	her in Copenhagen.
18	Dad's boss	isn't going to be • 8 aren't going to be • 2	here on Thursday.
19	The teachers	is going to have • 19 are going to have • 22	a meeting.
20	My older brother	is going to lend • 23 are going to lends • 1	me his Bravo magazine.
21	I	am going to spend • 19 am go to spending • 21	all my money on comics.
22	Martina	am going to wear • 6 is going to wear • 15	a dress to the party tonight.
23	Wild Bill	is going to sells • 3 is going to sell • 24	his old horse.
24	I	am going to write • 20 is going to write • 18	a letter tomorrow.

Don't Eat on the Bus!

Find the correct tense!

Die Abkürzungen haben folgende Bedeutung: pres. prog. = Present Progressive; sim. pres. = Simple Present; sim. past = Simple Past; pres. perf. = Present Perfect; "going to" fut. = "going to" Future

1   Kevin and Kathy have decided to go shopping today.
    "going to" fut. | 3   sim. past | 12   pres. perf. | 7

2   Kathy needs a bell for her bike.
    sim. past | 21   sim. pres. | 5   pres. perf. | 17

3   Kevin is going to buy a yo-yo.
    sim. pres. | 2   "going to" fut. | 16   pres. prog. | 23

4   They take a bus into the city centre.
    sim. past | 15   sim. pres. | 2   pres. perf. | 1

5   The bus is stopping at a red light.
    sim. pres. | 10   pres. prog. | 4   "going to" fut. | 13

6   The traffic light has just turned green.
    pres. perf. | 12   sim. past | 16   pres. prog. | 8

7   The bus hasn't left yet.
    sim. pres. | 19   pres. perf. | 17   sim. past | 22

8   What on earth is wrong?
    pres. perf. | 11   sim. past | 14   simp. pres | 1

9   Someone has caused a traffic-jam!
    pres. perf. | 15   sim. pres. | 3   sim. past | 24

10   Kevin wanted to get out of the bus.
    sim. pres. | 17   sim. past | 3   pres. perf. | 6

11   Kathy said it was too dangerous.
    sim. past | 14   pres. perf. | 20   pres. prog. | 1

12   The passengers are becoming quite angry.
    pres. prog. | 6   sim. past | 4   sim. pres. | 11

13   An old lady is shaking her umbrella at the traffic-jam.
    pres. perf. | 5   pres. prog. | 19   sim. past | 23

14 She is going to get out of the bus.
pres. perf. | 10   pres. prog. | 16   "going to" fut. | 11

15 She has decided to end the traffic-jam.
sim. past | 2   pres. perf. | 22   "going to" fut. | 8

16 She looks round and sees the problem at once.
sim. pres. | 8   sim. past | 4   pres. perf. | 15

17 A young man drove a sportscar into an ice-cream van.
sim. pres. | 17   sim. past | 23   pres. perf. | 1

18 Many boxes of ice-cream are lying everywhere.
sim. pres. | 3   pres. perf. | 7   pres. prog. | 21

19 The old lady runs back to the bus.
pres. cont. | 9   pres. perf. | 10   sim. pres. | 18

20 "Who wants to earn an ice-cream?"
sim. past | 24   sim. pres. | 13   pres. perf. | 16

21 All the children run out and help pick up the ice-cream.
sim. pres. | 9   pres. perf. | 7   pres. prog. | 12

22 They have already pushed the van and car off the road.
pres. perf. | 24   sim. past | 4   sim. pres. | 5

23 The traffic is beginning to move on now.
pres. prog. | 20   "going to" fut. | 9   pres. perf. | 17

24 They get their reward – all the ice-cream they can eat!
pres. perf. | 1   pres. prog. | 22   sim. pres. | 10

Signal Words:
Can You Find the Correct Answer?

Tip: *Achte auf die Zeitform!*

		tomorrow	14
1	Bill has **?** done his homework.	just	9
2	**?** he is running outside.	Last week	10
		Now	7
3	The ice-cream van left ten minutes **?** .	always	20
		ago	12
4	Fat Freddy **?** buys ice-cream for two.	ever	19
		always	10
5	Sue is going to give me a present **?** .	yesterday	24
		tomorrow	17
6	The baker makes hot rolls **?** .	every morning	20
		ago	2
7	Have you **?** been in a jumbo jet?	ever	1
		last week	15
8	The police have **?** arrested the robber.	yet	5
		already	3
9	Our dog drank my father's beer **?** .	since	4
		last night	23
10	A mouse fell into the beer two minutes **?** .	for	13
		ago	6
11	He is going to stop drinking beer **?** .	tomorrow	4
		yet	24
12	Did Mandy sing **?** ?	last night	14
		always	1
13	She usually sings **?** afternoon.	every	21
		already	18
14	Cindy hasn't talked to her brother **?** Monday.	ago	6
		since	19
15	I haven't been to China **?** .	every day	17
		yet	11
16	I have **?** been to Spain.	yet	21
		never	22
17	Have you **?** been to Spain?	ever	13
		yet	2
18	Willy **?** causes a lot of trouble.	yesterday	12
		always	24
19	Yvonne let the cat in ten minutes **?** .	ago	2
		yet	8
20	She is letting the dog in **?** .	ago	17
		at this moment	15
21	The dog has already found two bones **?** .	just	9
		today	5
22	The plane has **?** landed.	yesterday	19
		just	8
23	The flowers began to grow **?** .	yesterday	16
		every morning	17
24	Dinosaurs **?** love to eat flowers.	now	4
		always	18